Dead Sure?

I dedicate this book to Michael and Yoma Rees, my good friends, supporters, encouragers and in-laws.

Dead Sure?

about yourself, life, faith

J. John

f r a m e w o r k s

FRAMEWORKS
38 De Montfort Street,
Leicester LE1 7GP,
England

© J. John 1989
First published 1989
Reprinted 1991, 1992, 1993

Distributed in Australia by ANZEA Publishers,
Australian ISBN 0-85892-400-5

British Library Cataloguing in Publication Data
John J. (John)
  Dead sure?
  1. Jesus Christ
  I. Title II. Series
232

ISBN 0-85110-670-6

Set in Baskerville
Photoset in Great Britain by Parker Typesetting Service, Leicester
Design and illustration by Spring Graphics, Saintfield, N. Ireland
Printed in Great Britain by Bath Press Colourbooks, Glasgow

FRAMEWORKS is an imprint of Inter-Varsity Press, the book-publishing division of the Universities and Colleges Christian Fellowship.

Contents

. . . a rescue act, reaching down to the deepest point of our need.

Acknowledgments

I would like to thank my assistant Ric Thorpe for helping me revise the original manuscript of this book. Ric, you are an inspiration!

Thanks also to Dave Male and David Stone for reading through it and giving helpful comments. Thanks to Jackie Maugham for all the typing. Many thanks to Tony and Denise Molyneux for providing a computer and a home in Australia to finish the book. G'day!

Thanks to Peggy Wright, Dorinda Miller and all in our prayer group; to Ian and Lorraine, our neighbours, who keep feeding me with ideas (you'd better read this!); and to my dear friends Lois Thompson and Sue Garmen who keep me down to earth. Thank you, Michael (my eighteen-month-old son), for tearing up some of my notes, and Killy, my wife, my closest, honest friend.

chapter one

Life story

No-one who reads the newspaper or hears the news needs persuading that we have problems.

When we hear news of a peace treaty, we think that progress is being made. But during the last century over 9,000 peace treaties have

been signed, many of them just torn to pieces afterwards. In the cause of peace we even go to war and fight! In spite of recent international summit meetings there is still a real threat of nuclear war – and if not war then maybe a nuclear disaster following a power-station accident or a terrorist attack. As one graffiti artist has commented, 'If you've seen one nuclear war, you've seen them all.'

Certainly uncertain

Yet everyone, from weathermen to the world's stockbrokers, tries to assure us that all is well. But, going on their past record, can we really have much faith in them? In October 1987 the weather forecast proved to be seriously false. The unprepared-for storms not only wrecked homes, cars and trees but also took twenty-two lives. In the same month the money markets of the world crashed in a matter of days. Millions of pounds were wiped off the Stock Exchange. Security turned into insecurity in minutes as some even became bankrupt. The only fundamental certainty is fundamental uncertainty.

At the same time millions of people are

starving all round the world. An estimated 25,000 starve to death every day. For many of us, this problem seems far away from our homes where we comfortably sit and over-eat. These people are only 'statistics', though, aren't they? And, of course, statistics don't bleed.

We are all agreed that these are major issues in the world today. Many people are concerned about them, having a genuine desire to solve them. Comedian Ben Elton believes that 'we change the world by electing governments who act for the good of the people of the country, not for the paymasters. I don't know how we go about that.' Governments do their best. 'But governments don't solve problems, they merely rearrange them,' as Ronald Reagan said once.

New Musical Express,
17 October 1987.

And our advertisers do not even try to solve them. They just pretend they don't exist and invite us into a dream world of cosmetics, clothes and cars. If we do allow ourselves to look more closely at these problems and delve deeper in our search for their solutions, we find that they are merely symptoms of a far deeper problem.

What or who is the main problem? Society, the government, capitalism, socialism, the weather? No.

We must be honest with ourselves. *We* are the main problem. *People* cause wars. *People* control the money markets. *People* hold on to excess food and make decisions not to share it. Canadian singer Bruce Cockburn said, 'This is my trouble. Can't be an innocent bystander in a world of pain and fire and steel.' Now it's not that these problems don't concern us, it's just that we've got enough problems of our own.

Inner City Front, RCA
Records, 1981.

Search for the truth

Modern jazz-rock singer Joe Jackson remarked once, 'Some days I look in the mirror and think,

"What a waster. I might as well go back to bed and die."' Do you ever feel like that? What is wrong with us?

As we begin to take off the masks which cover up most of our lives, we uncover feelings of unhappiness, despair, lack of purpose and difficulties in our closest relationships. One factor that causes a lot of anguish in our lives is that we try to ignore these things. When we find them confronting us we try to push them back down again, as if they don't exist. Is it no surprise then that we sometimes feel the way we do, with all those things stored up inside?

American singer Bruce Springsteen put it in a song:

'I get up in the morning
And I ain't got nothing to say
I come home in the evening
I go to bed feeling the same way
I ain't nothing but tired
Man, I'm just tired and bored with myself . . .'

Born in the USA, CBS Records, 1984.

Many are constantly feeling swayed this way and that. We talk about what we want from life – to graduate successfully, to get a good job, to fall in love, to marry and to have a family. But it soon becomes clear that we are really only describing what our parents, our teachers and our employers expect of us rather than what we want ourselves. And even if our parents tell us that we have the freedom to make our own decisions, we soon realize that that just makes our situation even more difficult, since we have so little conviction about our own goals.

Voices in the night

One person expressed this state of affairs by saying, 'I'm just a collection of mirrors, reflecting what everyone else expects of me.'

The dream of a young woman illustrates this dilemma. She had had many partners, but she wanted to get married and could not choose between two possible men. One man was the steady, middle-class type, of whom her well-to-

This is my trouble. Can't be an innocent bystander.

do family would have approved. The other shared her artistic and musical interests. In the course of deciding she could not make up her mind as to what kind of person she really was and what kind of life she wished to lead. She dreamed that a large group of friends took a vote on which of the two men she should marry. During the dream she felt relieved. This was certainly a convenient solution. The only trouble was that when she awoke, she couldn't remember which way the vote had gone!

I'm invisible

Many people who have gone steady or lived together are deeply scared at having to split up. Others who have marriage plans can't go through with them. And many who are married are dissatisfied with their partner. They eventually realize that their expectations of each other (real or hoped-for) are more than they should have been. They expect them to fill

Any suggestions?

... suddenly freed from uncertainty and the boredom of labour.

There must be some solution to how we're feeling. So what is it? At the beginning of the twentieth century, the psychologist Sigmund Freud wrote that the most common cause of such problems was our difficulty in accepting the sexual side of life and the conflict between sexual impulses and social taboos. Was he right?

In the 1930s, the sociologist Karen Horney wrote that the root cause of our problems was hostility between individuals and groups all seeking to get ahead of each other. Was she right?

Many people dream of sudden riches, obtained by chance or by the exercise of skill. They dream of being suddenly freed from uncertainty and the boredom of labouring for their daily needs. Lotteries and the numerous some desperate vacuum within themselves and they get angry or resentful when this doesn't happen.

It's great when we hear about a successful marriage or news of two who have fallen in love. But when we look at what we ourselves have been through we begin to wonder how long things will last. Many of us have had shattering experiences with people we have been very close to. Circumstances go wrong, relationships fall apart, and we're left to pick up the pieces. Alison Moyet's song 'Invisible' sums up what it's like to be on the wrong side of some relationships.

> 'Invisible
> I feel like I'm invisible
> You treat me like I'm not really there
> And you don't really care.'

Many expect others to fill some desperate vacuum within . . . and get angry when this doesn't happen.

Alf, CBS Records. 1984.

variations of gambling have long catered for this need. What about this one?

William Hearst, a multi-millionaire, thought the solution was money. He amassed great power and wealth. But he was so anxious underneath this appearance of strength, particularly with regard to dying, that he wouldn't allow anyone to use the word 'death' in his presence. He was so anxious he didn't even have time to enjoy life.

In the 1970s Ian Dury and his band, the Blockheads, told us 'Sex and drugs and rock and roll. That is all my body wants.' Is that the solution?

Are these the solutions to how we're really feeling? Or are they just roads to a deeper problem?

Mantelpiece collection

One of the major problems of people today is loneliness. Loneliness is a feeling of not being significant, of not counting, of not mattering to anyone. There is no essential connection between feeling lonely and being alone. A person can feel very lonely and yet be in a crowd. A person can be physically alone and yet have a strong feeling of personal value.

Sometimes when I visit homes for the aged I sense that many feel lonely. They must occasionally feel that they don't count, that they don't matter, that they are not significant. When people age and the shadow of death becomes more and more real, the threat of loneliness can be severe and can be rivalled only by a fear of death.

Some of my friends emphasize how crucial it is for them to be invited to a particular party or dinner – not because they especially want to go (though they do go), or because they will get enjoyment, companionship, or sharing of experience in the gathering. (Very often they do not, but are simply bored.) Rather, being invited is crucial because it proves that they are wanted and that they are not alone. The mantelpiece collection of invitations no longer seems to serve as just a reminder, but as a statement saying, 'People like me. You just look how many things people want me to go to.'

Being invited is crucial . . .

World-famous pop singer Rod Stewart tells us, 'Most days I wish I was dead except for the three hours a night I'm on stage.'

The great physicist Albert Einstein, in a letter to a friend, wrote: 'It is strange to be known so universally and yet to be so lonely.'

Mother Teresa of Calcutta remarked recently on television: 'The greatest disease today is not starvation. The greatest killer is loneliness.'

How do you feel?

But some parties can make you feel worse! At a party you can suddenly feel left out or not part of the group. Sometimes long standing friendships become questionable. Why should this happen at a party? It must be that the expected joyousness is not experienced and this allows other feelings to take over.

Loneliness reveals to us our most radical need, our deepest drive, our most important desire. Loneliness tells us that to be a person we must love and be loved. The fact that we feel we don't matter to anyone suggests that we know we *ought* to matter. The feeling of loneliness suggests that life ought not to be like this. We feel the need to be loved. So the experience of being loved, of knowing that someone cares for you, that you matter to someone, is probably the best cure for loneliness. John Lydon, former member of the Sex Pistols, said, 'Of all things, I cry from loneliness, maybe.'

The feeling of loneliness suggests that life ought not to be like this.

Road to nowhere

No-one who watches the world through the morning newspaper or the evening TV news needs to be persuaded that we live in an age of anxiety. We so often give the impression that everything is fine. It's all right. We will be OK. But history is full of dramatic and often devastating events that have left their scars.

More than forty years ago the first atomic bomb blew up over Japan, killing 87,000 people. Now forty nations in the world have nuclear weapons. One single missile has fifteen times the explosive power of all the bombs that fell in the last World War. The scientist Albert Einstein wrote: 'When we released the energy from the atom, everything changed except our way of thinking, and so we drift towards unparalleled disaster.'

The anxiety that this is causing has led to massive anti-nuclear protest movements the world over. What is perhaps the most disconcerting element is that the issue seems so far beyond our control.

What is anxiety?

Anxiety may be mild tension before an interview, or worry before an examination, because the future is at stake. Or it may be someone's forehead dripping with sweat, waiting to hear whether a lover has been lost in a plane crash. People experience anxiety in all sorts of ways – a 'gnawing' within, general bewilderment or even sheer terror, such as a child might experience when she suddenly realizes she is lost. That is anxiety. In its full-blown intensity, anxiety can be the most painful emotion we experience.

What are the answers? How can we avoid these problems? In the race against time, is it possible to solve the hassles in our lives? Or is it a case of like it or lump it?

The missing link

As we keep on looking for the solutions to our problems, we begin to see that whatever we try, it just doesn't pass the test. We seem to be filling ourselves with something which turns out to be rubbish. When we realize that what we thought could have been the answer, is not, we are left in despair. Our search, conscious or not, continues.

The hollow men

Many people today could echo, in their own experience, the words T. S. Eliot wrote in 1925:

'We are the hollow men
We are the stuffed men
Learning together
Headpiece filled with straw. Alas!
Shape without form, shade without colour,
Paralysed force, gesture without motion . . .'

The Hollow Men, in
Collected Poems, Faber,
1974.

But there is something missing. We remain empty. It's as if there is some gap or void in our lives that needs to be filled with the right thing. That's what we feel when we are lonely. That's what we feel when we are plagued by anxiety. That's what we feel when we are going nowhere. Bruce Cockburn puts it well:

> 'There must be more . . . more
> More current, more spark
> More touch deep in the heart
> Not more thoughtless cruelty
> Not more being this lonely.'

Humans, Pläne Records, 1980.

When people tell of a break-up of a love-relationship, they don't so much say that they feel sorrow, but rather that they feel empty. The loss of the other has left an inner void. When someone does not know what he wants or what he feels, in a time of traumatic change, he discovers that the goals he had been taught to follow no longer bring him any security, or give him any sense of direction. He feels an inner void and senses danger. His natural reaction is to look around for other people. He hopes he will give him some sense of direction, or at least some comfort in the knowledge that he is not alone. John Lydon of the Sex Pistols says, 'Some people need cheap sex, instant selfish gratification. Fine. But it makes me more miserable than ever.'

New Musical Express,
10 October 1987.

All man's history

In response to the first atom-bomb explosion, over Hiroshima, Norman Cousins wrote an article in *Time* magazine entitled 'Man is Obsolete'. It's interesting that Mr Cousins did not write about how to protect oneself from atomic radiation, or how to meet political problems, or the tragedy of man's self-destruction. Instead, his article was about loneliness. 'All man's history' he wrote, 'is an endeavour to shatter his loneliness.'

I believe that this is our root problem. Everything seems to point to the fact that there is something missing. We try to fill it with things which just don't fit.

What is supposed to fill that gap?

Anxiety. Despair. Loneliness. Emptiness. Is death our only escape?

chapter two

Are you dead sure?

'Death is the ultimate statistic. One out of one dies.' That's how George Bernard Shaw summed up the whole issue of death. It is the stark fact that no-one can hide from. Is death the only escape from the emptiness that some of us feel? Does it hold the key to filling that gap?

We seldom hear anyone say of a loved one's death, 'It was normal.' We feel that the person's death could have been postponed. Death is something so strange that, in spite of our awareness of it, we don't really think it is going to happen to the ones we love. It always surprises us as something unbelievable.

There is no human experience that frightens us so much as death. The shadow of death raises some of the most important questions in life. What, if anything, does my life mean? Is there any goal or purpose to my life? Is all human existence meaningless, or is it, as Shakespeare's Macbeth said, 'sound and fury, signifying nothing'?

Some people, unable to cope with death, hit upon the idea of not thinking about it at all in order to be 'happy'. During the 1960s one of the characteristics attributed to large groups of people in Britain was a lack of interest in the subject – not just a lack of belief in life after death, but lack of interest in the question whether death was the end of human existence.

It's easy for us to feel that death is so far off that it's not worth thinking about. But eventually the shadow of death falls on us when someone close to us dies and we are forced to face the whole subject. Whatever conclusions

Death always surprises us as something unbelievable.

19

we do reach about death colour our entire life.

It's just a big con

One family doctor in a north London practice described how even doctors are scared to look death in the face. He explained to the *Guardian* newspaper that doctors' training is to do with saving life, and when a patient is terminally ill the barriers go up and the doctor tends to withdraw and stop physical contact. 'The dying patient on the ward round illustrates the point', he explained. 'It's just a big con and everyone joins in. The patient knows that the doctors find it difficult so he pretends to be asleep, and those doing the "round" say that it would be better not to disturb Mr So-and-so as he's asleep, and it avoids confrontation with difficult feelings and emotions.'

It is because of fear that some of us avoid the questions posed by death. We are too scared to think about it because we do not know what it has in store for us. If death is the end, does all that we have, and all that we are, just cease? And if death isn't the end, what is beyond that

> **Our conclusions about death colour our entire life.**

Everyone's got a hunger,
A hunger they can't resist.
There's so much that you want,
You deserve much more than this.

Bruce Springsteen, *Born to Run*, CBS Records, 1986.

we cannot see? The paradox is that Death may be the most illuminating experience we can consider in our efforts to find the meaning of human life.

The Greek philosopher Plato defined life as 'an apprenticeship for death'. He recommended meditation on death in order to discover the meaning of life.

Death rocks the mourners

Whether the deceased is a six-year-old or a sixty-year-old, death rocks the mourners. The question 'Why?' naturally arises. Death seems to be a mistake, an error. Plants and animals die, and that seems natural; but *people* shouldn't die.

Something leaves the body . . . what?

Shakespeare's King Lear voiced a universal human reaction to death. With his deceased daughter in his arms, he said,

> 'No, no, no life!
> Why should a dog, a horse, a rat have life
> And thou no breath at all?'

King Lear, V.iii.

But while King Lear says 'No' to death, others say 'Yes', and commit suicide. Thousands of people just cannot cope with life and they choose to end it themselves. These heart-breaking cases cause us even more discomfort. Sometimes we find the whole thing embarrassing because they haven't been able to cope with the everyday stresses of life. 'They couldn't handle it', some people say, assuming that the suicide victims are in some way inferior. But surely one of their reasons for taking their lives is because they believe that life is, after all, pointless. Are they right, or did they end it all before seeing what life really means?

We say people die. But what does death mean? The *Concise Oxford Dictionary* defines death in very simple terms. It is the 'final cessation of vital functions'. But perhaps that is too simple because it says nothing of the suffering that many go through on their way to death. Today it is still seldom a short and painless thing. It may be comforting to hope with Tennessee Williams that 'death is one moment and life so many of them', but such a conception is false. For many people, death comes only at the end of an agonizing illness, the outcome of which has been clearly written on the wall for years.

// **Death seems to be a mistake. Plants and animals die, and that seems natural; but *people* shouldn't die!** //

'There's a hole in my life.'

The Police.

The facts of death

In Elizabethan times, life expectancy was a little over thirty-five years. By Queen Victoria's time it was about sixty-five. Today, due to modern

Suicidal

Just over 100,000 people throughout the world commit suicide every year, for a variety of reasons and using a variety of methods ranging from the unremarkable to the bizarre. Despite the statistical and other information available today, our understanding of suicide has not advanced greatly. Most of the questions asked in research are inevitably directed to those who have failed in the attempt. It is true to say that the greater the flow of information and the more detailed it is, the less successful are our efforts to understand suicide. But the 100,000 people who do succeed in committing suicide each year must be saying something.

Why have they given up on life? Have they found that life is pointless after all? Or have they just missed seeing the answer?

surgery and the development of pharmacology, it is seventy-five. Death may be delayed a little, but our end will be the same.

To put the matter simply, the facts of death are that an individual's heart stops beating and his brain stops functioning. A doctor looks at such an individual and says, 'He is dead.' All that the doctor can say, as a doctor, is that the physical signs that we associate with human life are no longer present. The next person to be contacted is the undertaker so that the corpse may be buried or cremated according to the practices of a particular society.

The atheist (someone who believes there is no God) looks at the evidence that the doctor offers him and believes that because the body no longer lives, the 'person' no longer lives. An important point to stress is that the atheist's view of death is no less an act of faith than the Christian's. The atheist cannot go beyond death to prove that death is the end of everything. But he does actually go beyond the evidence and believes something that cannot be proven by the evidence available.

> **With death so inevitable in our lives, surely we must get serious about it . . .**

The ultimate question

The ancient Greeks were puzzled by death. They weighed a body just before death and then straight after death. Of course, the weight was the same. But 'something' had left the body! What was it?

There is more to us than flesh and bone. We have feelings, we have thoughts and we have a will. They're not physical but they certainly exist. What happens to them when we die? Do they just vanish?

Whether death is the end or whether there is an 'afterlife', we all agree that we shall all die. We just do not know when that will be. The inevitability of death and our uncertain hold on this life are two major causes of our deep-seated anxiety concerning death.

Can you handle it?

The author and professor, C. S. Lewis, wrote after the death of his wife:

> 'An odd by-product of my loss is that I'm aware of being an embarrassment to everyone I meet. At work, at the club, in the street, I see people, as they approach me, trying to make up their minds whether they'll "say something about it" or not. . . . Some . . . walk up to me as if I were a dentist, turn very red, get it over and then edge away to the bar as quickly as they decently can.'

C. S. Lewis, *A Grief Observed*, Faber & Faber, 1961.

We cannot ignore death. So, in the light of death, what is life? Seriously to think about life only when death seems imminent is not a good time to deal with the issue. Business people will always take prudent measures in ample time to acquire financial gains. A person on trial for his life would be stupid if he didn't prepare for his trial before the day of the trial itself. In the same way we must think about our destiny now rather than delay until we are on our deathbeds.

We cannot give a meaning to life unless we give a meaning to death. Death can have meaning if life has meaning. The two cannot be separated. If you're not sure about death, are you sure you know what life is all about? With death as such an obvious and inevitable conclusion to our lives, surely we must get serious about it at some time or another.

Are you dead sure about the way you're going in life? Are you dead sure that death is the end? Are you dead sure that you've got the answers?

. . . sometime.

chapter three

Who's mad?

As we look around at mankind there is much that excites our wonder. Our great-great-grandparents would be amazed at what we have accomplished. The spectrum of achievement is broad, from transplant operations to probes into deep space.

Key questions

What is there that we cannot do? We have conquered Everest. We have begun to solve the mysteries of the universe. Life expectancy has increased along with improved living standards since the last century. Many people do try to live good lives, and by and large they succeed. We regularly hear of marriage breakdown, but many marriages (the ones we don't read about in newspapers) hold fast with honour, faithfulness and love. Millions live in peace and harmony with those around them. Indeed, the sacrifices made by ordinary people and their devotion to ideals and values prompt us to emphasize that there is good in mankind. We still have enough 'health' left in us to perceive that we are not 'healthy'.

So of all the many questions we can ask about ourselves, none is more important than the question 'What are we here for?'

Someone may argue that all we are here for is to look after Number One because life has no moral purpose. But let a burglar kill Number One's parents in the course of a robbery with violence, and Number One will be quick to say he shouldn't have done it – a moral judgment!

On the one hand, each of us is just one object in the universe, one creature among many. Yet on the other hand, we are more than just objects, for we alone are aware that there is

There is no doubt that we have an insatiable drive to find some dominating value in life.

morality, loneliness, emptiness, anxiety and the prospect of death in our lives. In some ways we may well be like other animals, but we are different. As far as we know, the hippopotamus doesn't discuss with his fellow hippopotamuses, 'Who am I?'

Yet as we study the vastness and wonder of the universe, we become more and more conscious of our own smallness on this planet.

Emil Brunner, in his book *Man in Revolt*, put his paradox in a single sentence: 'Man dreams of eternity and creates eternal works and then the loss of a little thyroid gland makes him an idiot.'

So what is the purpose of life? Who are we? Do we have an identity or are we meaningless?

What model is your car, brother?

The problem of our identity is bound up with our relationship to God. People are not sure who they are because they have lost contact with the one who gives them identity and meaning in life.

There is no doubt that we have an insatiable drive to find some object for worship, some dominating value in life. For some it is money, for others prestige, and for others acceptance. The list is long. The need to fill our lives with something becomes more and more pressing. Joy Davidman recognized one 'idol' in her book *Smoke on the Mountain*. She humorously put it this way:

> 'I worship a Rolls Royce sports model, brother.
>
> All my days I give it offerings of oil and polish.
>
> Hours of my time are devoted to its ritual, and it brings me luck in all my undertakings; and it establishes me among my fellows as a success in life.
>
> What model is your car, brother?'

We have the power of making moral choices, and on this power hang infinite possibilities for

As far as we know, the hippopotamus doesn't discuss with his fellow hippopotamuses, 'Who am I?'

Some want scientific proof before they will accept that God exists.

good or ill. The more we choose to place ourselves at the centre of life, the lower we place humanity. True humanism lies where God, and not man, is at the centre of all. We have the power to take moral decisions, and this makes us fundamentally different from animals.

G. K. Chesterton remarked: 'If I wish to dissuade a man from drinking his tenth whisky and soda, I slap him on the back and say "Be a man." No-one who wished to dissuade a crocodile from eating its tenth explorer would slap it on the back and say "Be a crocodile"!'

God and the Russians

So was there a God, and did he die, or did we die to God? Has anyone ever asked you what you believe? If not, I'm asking you now. What do you believe? We cannot escape the question of God. One has to take up *some* position on the matter. Some people are atheists. The atheist denies the existence of God. The agnostic claims that you cannot know whether there is a God. And if there is a God, so what? He can have little interest or influence in the world or in me as an individual.

The Soviet cosmonaut Yuri Gagarin, the first man to orbit the Earth, reported rather triumphantly that he found no God out there. But many people, in different times and countries, *have* claimed to have found God. The conclusion for some is that God does not exist and those who think they have met him are suffering from a delusion.

Looking for God by exploring space is like seeing all of Shakespeare's plays in the hope that you will find Shakespeare. Shakespeare is in one sense present at every moment in every play, but he is not present in the same way as the characters on the stage.

Some people get so caught up in the enjoyment of a play that they almost seem to forget who actually wrote it. In the same way, some people are so busy enjoying God's creation that they forget to acknowledge that there is a God behind it all.

The three-letter word 'God' conjures up all sorts of ideas to people today. To many, the word represents someone unknown. To some it is a word to be feared. But to those who know God intimately, the name brings to mind thoughts of love, goodness, mercy and of an ever-present Friend.

Science-fiction faith

The science-fiction film *2001 – A Space Odyssey* focuses repeatedly on an impersonal black slab that appears in space, compelling a sense of mystery and awe. It is evidently a symbol of some superhuman power.

Some people think of God in terms of some such monumental black rock, looming large and inert. God is not like that black slab at all. He is personal and very much alive and well.

But how do we know? Some atheists maintain that the evidence of science proves that there is no God. Some agnostics want scientific proof before they will accept that God exists.

A group was discussing Christianity and one person said, 'I was raised on the scientific method and no-one has ever been able to prove to me scientifically that God exists.'

A Christian responded, 'Your problem is similar to one of my own. I was raised on the theological method and no-one has ever been able to prove to me theologically that an atom exists.'

'But whoever heard of finding an atom by theology?' exclaimed the sceptic.

'Exactly,' the Christian answered.

We limit ourselves if we look at God purely in terms of science.

> **To tackle the issue of God's existence purely scientifically just does not work.**

God is dead.

Nietzsche is dead.

Nietzsche

God

Leap in the dark

One student said that he had had his eyes opened about the fantasy of faith in God. When asked what he thought faith was he said: 'It is believing the unbelievable, accepting something for which there is no proof. It is a blind leap in the dark.'

Is faith in God really a blind leap in the dark? No. Faith in God is based on evidence as surely as science is; the difference is in the kind of evidence on which each is based. If I took a rose and said, 'The rose is red,' that would be a statement for which there is scientific evidence. But suppose I said, 'The rose is beautiful.' That statement cannot be tested scientifically. But is it not still true?

I can't believe

'I just couldn't put up with that cycle of things where you just grow up, get a job, get married and die. Maybe this is where Christ comes in, as far as my life is concerned. Because I can't believe we just appeared here out of gas. I can't believe that, and maybe that's where my spiritual nature comes from, that fight. For wanting to break out of that type of conventionalism.'

Bono of U2, March 1982. Quoted in Steve Turner, *Hungry for Heaven*, Virgin, 1988.

These stories illustrate a simple problem: people with different starting-points communicate in different ways. For example, in scientific terms a kiss is 'the approach of two pairs of lips with a reciprocal transmission of microbes and carbon dioxide'. Now, is that what comes to your mind when you kiss someone? No, a kiss is a personal experience which is completely lost when it is described in any other way.

Similarly we cannot define God in scientific terms, expecting a computer print-out to give the final proof of his existence. To tackle the issue of God's existence purely scientifically or mathematically just does not work. We must have another way of approaching the issue, because he is personal.

The God of the Bible is not a dead concept from the distant past. He is alive. He is unique. He is creative and brings things to life. To encounter God is to enter into something real, giving us a deepening awareness of life.

Prove your knowledge!

What do you do if you tell someone something you know to be true, and they say, 'I don't believe you. Prove it!'?

Can you? If you try you will have problems. You will have to base your 'proof' on one of three types of knowledge: mathematical, scientific, or personal.

The first is mathematical knowledge. Take the statement $2+2=4$. It is logical, and the knowledge contained in the statement can be built up from simple, reasoned statements.

The second is scientific knowledge. This is acquired when a hypothesis is proposed and tested or verified by repeated experiments until the knowledge gained is beyond reasonable doubt.

The third type is personal knowledge. This is experiental. I know that something is true because I saw it or have experienced it. If I love someone, I cannot prove it mathematically or scientifically but I know it is true. If I meet someone, there is no way I can prove to you scientifically that I have actually done so if you weren't there at the time! Try it.

Because God is personal, mathematical and scientific categories are inadequate to describe him.

But what about all the things we don't understand?

We get off to a bad start when we try to assess God as we would anyone else. We cannot 'psych' God out. If you and I could understand God he wouldn't be worth believing in. He's greater than all of our minds put together.

God is a mystery to be enjoyed, not a problem to be solved. Rather than a riddle which alienates us, God should be a mystery that fascinates and beckons. This is the sense of wonder that one of the writers of the New Testament captures: 'Oh, the depth of the riches of the wisdom and knowledge of God! How unsearchable his judgments, and his paths beyond tracing out! To him be the glory for ever' (*Romans, chapter 11, verses 33–36*).

God cannot be boxed into the narrow confines of our expectations. God is different and delightfully so!

The God of the Bible confirmed by my experience is truth wrapped in surprise and wonder. God delights in the unexpected and the unlikely. Anyone who wants to be in touch with this creative, living God has to let go of the conventional values that prize power, profits and pride of intellect. I find it amazing that God (so highly unconventional) allows me to be his friend. I thought I was smart when I was an agnostic, but I had to learn that 'getting smart' consisted of realizing that there was a God whom I could know.

There is no-one as together as God. God is authentic, being simply what he is – 'for real'. God is sheer integrity. God is wholesome. Words cannot be found to explain him and yet he is a person. That means he doesn't treat me like one among millions; because he is personal, he relates to me personally – if I allow him.

The Bible makes it clear that mere knowledge *about* God is not the same as knowledge *of* God. Knowing things about a person is not the same as knowing that person.

It is possible to acknowledge that God exists without having a relationship with God; to know about God and yet not to know him. The Bible reveals that we can know God personally, and shows us how to set about getting to know him.'

God is not dead! Alexander Solzhenitsyn recently said that 'men have forgotten God'. Thank God that he hasn't forgotten us.

//
We cannot 'psych' God out.
//

chapter four

Innocently guilty

'Drink Maxwell House coffee – it tastes so good it's sinful!' What is it about sin that moves people to buy products? 'Fresh cream cakes – naughty but nice!' How healthy is sin? For that matter what *is* sin?

Sin for most people is a rather vague idea until it crystallizes into some kind of crime. But then for some people crime is crime, and not sin – is it?

In a very interesting book called *Whatever Happened to Sin?*, Dr Karl A. Menninger tells of his disappointment with the results of psychiatry despite his high hopes when he began in that profession. He says:

'In the field of psychiatry, sin became a dirty word that was the scapegoat for most of our problems. It caused that guilt complex that was so detrimental to good mental health. So sin went into crime. We decided we would pass a law against it and then we wouldn't have to worry about sin anymore. Instead of outlawing sin, however, we have in-lawed it. We are accepting it.'

Dr Menninger's comments are rather perceptive. No-one likes to be called a sinner. We find the word offensive. So we use other, less threatening words. The adulterer is not called a sinner but is said to have a marital problem. The insider dealer fiddling the Stock Exchange is now called a victim of circumstances.

These descriptions are a cover-up for sin. Only as we face up to sin honestly can we find a remedy.

Because of all this there are many people who do not recognize their sins and therefore have an imperfect and inadequate idea of themselves.

I speak to many people who believe that they are innocent. I have even met people who have said that they have never sinned. But of course what they mean is 'I've never robbed a bank.' (Well, if you put it that way, I've never robbed a bank!) Or 'I've never murdered anybody.' (Well, I've never murdered anyone either!) Does that make them innocent? Others I have met believe they are 'Christian' because they keep the Ten Commandments. When asked to quote them, however, they just can't seem to recollect them! (Borrow a Bible and look them up in *Exodus, chapter 20, verses 1–17*.)

God's good guide

Of course the Ten Commandments are a good guide. The first four tell us how to love God and the last six show us how to love our neighbour.

One historian has said, 'Men and women are able creatures, but they have made 32,647,389 laws and haven't yet improved on the Ten Commandments!'

Let's test ourselves against the Ten Commandments.

1. Have we always put God at the centre of our life, where he ought to be?

2. Have we ever put anything else in the place of God in our life?

3. Have we ever taken the name of God carelessly upon our lips?

4. Have we always kept one day a week for special time with God and relaxation?

(One medical doctor, Sir James Crichton-Browne, has commented on this commandment: 'We doctors, in the treatment of nervous disorders, are constantly compelled to prescribe periods of rest. Some periods are, I think, only Sundays in arrears.')

5. Have we always respected and honoured our parents?

> Men and women have made 32,647,389 laws but haven't yet improved on the Ten Commandments!

35

6. Have we ever hated anyone, or become bitter and resentful?

7. Have we ever committed adultery? Jesus taught that to harbour impure, lustful thoughts about another person is to commit adultery in our heart.

8. Have we ever stolen or 'borrowed' anything, or used the firm's time or phone or equipment for our own purposes?

9. Have we ever told a lie or half-truth about another person?

10. Have we ever coveted what is not ours? Can we say we are innocent?

Missing the mark

The root meaning of the Greek word most often used for 'to sin' in the New Testament (it was written in Greek) is 'to miss' – to miss the mark, to fall short. And we keep falling short of the ideal, or missing the mark of perfect response, perfect choices, because there is so much within us, so much that is a part of what we are, which holds us back, drags us down, deflects us.

Christian writers in the past, in an effort to get specific about sin, identified seven roots of sin in us. They were called 'seven capital sins', seven headings under which sins can be classi-fied. They are *pride, anger, envy, greed, lust, laziness* and *gluttony*. They are destructive tend-encies in us.

Every generation has helped to make this world the place it is.

These should not be confused with their legitimate healthy counterparts: a good self-image (which is not pride), healthy anger, an energizing desire for achievement, recognition or love (which is not envy), normal acceptance of wealth and possessions (which is not greed), sexual desire (which is not lust), a delight in comfort, rest and food (which is neither laziness nor gluttony).

These 'seven capital sins' are destructive tendencies and drives in our being that have got twisted and are no longer pointed toward their legitimate, healthy goals. But they are not only the causes of sins we commit, they are also the effects of sin – not just of our own sins, but of the sins of the world. They are a self-destructiveness bequeathed to us by every previous generation of the human race.

'There are too many people pointing the finger, saying that you need to do this. But all the great writers that I respond to, be they in the Bible or otherwise, are people who said "we", as in "We need to get down on our knees. We need to turn about. We are going wrong."'

We too

Bono, March 1982, quoted in Steve Turner, *Hungry for Heaven.*

Poisons that kill us

Every generation that has preceded us has helped to make this world the place it is. Right now we are affecting the environment for ourselves and for those who will come after us. And much of what we are doing is destructive. By our sins we poison the world we and others must live in.

I am not talking about chemical poisons we inject into the air, the water and the earth, but the poisons we inject into one another when our behaviour is destructive.

How much have our exploitative words and actions over the ages contributed to turning healthy sexual desire into lust? How much of what we call 'competitiveness' is really envy or sheer greed, having become a destructive compulsion in us through the influence of countless words and actions great and small? As human beings we interact with one another and as we do so we affect one another. We condition one another's thinking, feeling and behaviour, sometimes in ways we are unable to reverse. Our sins leave their mark – both in individuals and on our culture. Like some of the substances which our industrial society is pouring into the atmosphere and seas or burying in the earth, our sins stay there. They don't simply dissolve without trace.

None of us escapes the influence of this. Before we are old enough to be guilty of any personal act of sin, destructive tendencies are

Someone else's fault

I went to my psychiatrist
To be psychoanalysed,
To find out why I killed the cat
And blacked my husband's eyes.

He laid me on a couch,
To see what he could find.
And here is what he dredged up,
From my subconscious mind.

When I was one my Mummy
Hid my dolly in a trunk,
And so it follows naturally
That I am always drunk.

When I was two I saw my father
Kiss the maid one day,
And that is why I suffer from
Kleptomania.

When I was three I had the feeling
Of ambivalence towards my brothers,
And so it follows naturally
I poisoned all my lovers.

But I am happy, now I've learnt
The lesson this has taught –
That everything that I do wrong
Is someone else's fault!

Anne Russell

39

formed within us and therefore destructive patterns of behaviour. Before we are old enough to know right from wrong we become skilful at responding to the aggressive, manipulative behaviour of other people with aggressive, manipulative tactics of our own. We were born into the middle of a catfight, and we find ourselves scratching and clawing in self-defence almost before our eyes are open.

So are we innocent or guilty?

Life on the big screen

I'm not trying to load guilt on to you as a kind of emotional blackmail. It wouldn't be right and wouldn't wash. All Christianity does is recognize guilt and wrong rather than pretend that it doesn't exist. We can sweep it under the carpet, but the dirt is still there. As U2 put it 'Sweet the sin, but bitter the taste in my mouth.'

Just in case you still are in doubt – one more illustration. Imagine the whole of your life projected on to a screen in front of you. It reveals everything you have done, everything you have said and everything you have ever thought. How would you feel at seeing it on your own? How would you feel at seeing it in the presence of everybody involved in the film as well? Some of it would be great. But all of it?

The heart of the problem

A man in court, pleading innocence, listened for several hours to the court proceedings and then shouted, 'I'm guilty!'

The judge turned to him and said, 'Why didn't you say that several hours ago?'

'Well,' replied the man, 'I didn't realize I was guilty till I heard all the evidence!'

The problems in the world will not be sorted out until we deal with the main problem. And the main problem is and always has been *us*. 'The heart of the human problem is the problem of the human heart.' Jesus Christ said that all these wrongs come from a person's heart.

'Out of the heart come evil thoughts, murder, adultery, sexual immorality, theft, false

" **A new heart is what I need.** "

U2, *War*, Island Records, 1983.

testimony, slander. These are what make a man unclean' (*Matthew 15:19–20*).

Or as Don Henley, a former member of the Eagles, put it, 'We have met the enemy – and he is us.'

Building the Perfect Beast, Geffen Records, 1984.

How did it start?

Sin originated when we turned our back on God. We were created in God's likeness to live in the world and to enjoy an intimate relationship with him. Because God is love we were not forced into this relationship; we were given the free will to choose, to accept or to reject God. But we have turned away from God.

This had the immediate effect of cutting us off from him. This is sin: shutting God out of our lives, independence from God. But we cannot ignore God without something going wrong. God is life and light.

Remove life, and death results. Remove light, and darkness is left. The loving relationship that God wanted us to have with him has been broken by sin. Sin became part of human nature and its tendencies have been passed from generation to generation. We all have a considerable overdraft of sin. Being 'good' does not pay off our overdraft.

Who can get us out of debt with God? Only someone with the spiritual resources to do so. And that someone must be one whom God recognizes and can represent us before him. He must be able to pay our debt and bring us back into contact with God.

The Bible calls this person 'the mediator' (1 Timothy 2:5) because he, Jesus Christ, God's Son, came into the world as a really human person to pay our debt and bring us back to God. He came to deal with that debt, our sin, that causes our breakdown of communication.

This is the background to Christianity. Whether you have consciously sinned or 'innocently' sinned – you and I have sinned and we both need a Saviour. Keep reading!

> We all have a considerable overdraft. Being 'good' does not pay off our overdraft.

chapter five

The suffering problem

How can there be a God when there is so much suffering?

In my work I travel around a lot and meet many people. Probably the most common question I am asked is something like this: 'How can there be a God when there is so much suffering in the world?'

This question, phrased in a variety of different ways, seems to be a real stumbling-block for some in accepting Christianity. And yet there are other people, like my friend Alyn Haskey who is a quadraplegic, who have found answers to this question and they are committed Christians.

What about me? Well, I have had my fair share of illness. I have known what it is to have personal tragedy, but I have not suffered as much as many people. Through all of this, however, it is good to remember that for every part of our body that goes wrong there are still hundreds that go right. And though we do all become very conscious of ill health when we are unwell, we should also be very conscious of good health when we have got it. But we are not. We just take it for granted.

Statistics that bleed

Television has communicated to us the suffering of a whole world in such large doses that many of us are becoming immune to it. We have seen so many pictures of starving African children that we almost switch off mentally. We can hear news of innocent people suffering and being killed in Beirut, and be deeply affected at first. But similar deaths a year later become just more statistics. There is so much suffering in the world that it is considered commonplace.

We should not just turn our backs on the problem of suffering. We must face it squarely and try to find the answers.

Christianity has no slick answer to suffering in the world. But if we look at what God has shown us we can go as far as we need to go to cope with the problem.

Why does God allow suffering?

Suffering is an acute problem to those who believe that there is a God who cares and can actually do something about it.

The problem is that there is only one God and he is good.

There would be no problem if there were many gods, because some might be good while others might be bad. But if there is only one good God, he must care.

And, being God, he has the power.to stop suffering. If God is as helpless as we are and says, 'I do sympathize but I can't do anything, I'm afraid,' then we have another problem! But it is because God is all-powerful, and therefore *could* stop things, that suffering is such a problem. If God does love us then surely he would want to spare us suffering.

It is because Christians believe in one God who is all-powerful and who cares for us that there is a question regarding suffering.

Here are some of the 'answers' people have suggested.

1. Some say that we suffer because we live in an imperfect world. If God had made the world perfect there would be no famines, earthquakes or sickness. God has done a bad job in creating the world we live in.

2. Another answer is that suffering is due to the selfishness and arrogance of men and women. If we spent more money on enterprises such as cancer research and education, rather than nuclear defence and space exploration, we might lessen the amount of suffering in the world a great deal.

According to the Bible all suffering is in the end due to sin. As we saw in the last chapter, sin is the root cause of all the chaos and suffering in the world.

But saying that all suffering is due to sin does not necessarily mean that whenever you suffer it's because you've done something wrong.

Sin now – pay later

If suffering is caused by sin, whose sin has caused it?

First of all, we bring some suffering upon ourselves by our own sins. For instance, if we squander our money on drugs, our brain cells are destroyed. If we drink excessive amounts of alcohol, we can expect liver damage. In these ways we cause our own suffering and destroy ourselves. The film title *Sin Now, Pay Later* sums up much of what we do. The Bible clearly informs us that what we sow we reap. So if we suffer later, it is wrong to blame God. We must blame only ourselves.

"
The world's inhumanity to its own people causes far more suffering than we care to admit.
"

Rape and poverty

Secondly, a great deal of the suffering in the world is caused by the sins or wrongs of others. A rapist leaves an innocent woman emotionally and physically distraught. War causes suffering for millions. The United Nations Food Organization says there is enough food in the world

for everybody. But not only do many of us eat more than we should; developed countries pile up food mountains instead of sharing their surpluses.

Is this type of suffering God's fault? No. We are in the wrong. The world's inhumanity to its own people causes far more suffering than we care to admit.

But it helps to realize that we live in a world which is not as God originally created it. It shares in the missing of the mark. It is dislocated, turned against us – a place of much suffering which reminds us forcibly that we cannot expect to live in a paradise when we have turned our backs on the Creator.

Now we can ask again: Why does God allow suffering? Why does God allow me to suffer for my own sins? Why does he allow me to live in a world in which there are earthquakes and droughts? And why does he allow me to suffer illness or the results of natural disasters?

Why does he allow me to suffer illness?

God sometimes allows me to suffer when *I* do something wrong so that I can learn from my mistakes. In our suffering he wants to teach us and warn us. Last Sunday morning's hangover, for instance, might be trying to tell you something about Saturday night's binge! If people always 'got away with it', can you imagine what life would be like?

But why should God allow me to suffer for somebody else's sin? This is a deeper question.

God did not make us to be isolated individuals, each living on our own desert island. He made us in such a way that we relate to one another and can help and love one another. But this fact holds out the possibility of hurting one another too. Would you rather God segregated us from one another so that we couldn't even help and be kind to one another?

Can suffering be good?

Why then does God allow the suffering we experience in a dislocated world? There is no simple answer to this question. One answer may be that it makes us think about life's meaning and purpose and our relationship to God. I do know that many a person struck by illness has begun to think about his or her life and destiny for the first time. Many people tend to be self-sufficient, till they hear God speak to them through suffering. Then they begin to see their insufficiency and sinfulness.

A Christian missionary, Mrs James Hudson Taylor, became blind towards the end of her life. Someone asked her, 'Why should you suffer after all the years of service doing things for God and for other people? Why should this happen to you?'

She replied, 'I suppose God wants to put the finishing touches to my character.'

It is often through pain and pressure that God can produce something very beautiful in our lives. We may not understand it (how much do we understand?), but knowing God personally enables us to trust him for allowing it.

Often beaten, never licked

We have looked at the causes of suffering and why God might allow it, but it is important not to ignore the fact that God is *ultimately* in control of suffering and that he is *intimately* involved in the suffering.

God is ultimately in control of suffering. He didn't just set the world in motion, winding it up like a clockwork toy and leaving it to wind down. If we allow him he can bring good out of the knocks in life. He can take suffering and produce something beautiful.

God does understand. God did an amazing thing in Jesus Christ. He identified with mankind. He entered our world and made himself vulnerable to our pain and suffering. Jesus suffered in a way that few of us suffer. He died a cruel, violent and painful death. God, who is ultimately in control of history, entered history, took human flesh, suffered, and died for his creation. He bore our guilt and our punishment. That is the extent of God's love. A

. . . produce something beautiful in our lives.

former Archbishop of Canterbury, William Temple, expressed it simply:

'There cannot be a God of love, Men say;
Because if there was and He looked on the world
His heart would break.
The Church points to the Cross and says it did break.
If God made the world, Men say, it's He who should bear the load.
The Church points to the Cross and says He did bear it.'

William Temple, *Readings in St John's Gospel*, Macmillan, 1961.

In the end it is not so much my suffering as my *reaction* to that suffering that really counts. If I am bitter and resentful in my suffering I still have my suffering, plus my bitterness and resentment. But if I yield myself to God in faith, my character can be refined. Samuel Rutherford, who suffered much for his faith, said, 'Grace grows best in winter.'

My story

Suffering is a real problem and we have no complete answer. I've struggled long and hard with this whole issue myself. Last week Mark, a close friend of mine, died of cancer. He was only twenty-seven. The same week the first baby of a couple we know died hours after a normal birth. A day later, another friend, Chris, died in a car crash on his way back from work, leaving a young wife.

Last week Mark, a close friend of mine, died of cancer.

But despite these personal tragedies, God is no less real to me. Despite the pain and confusion of suffering, we can still experience in Jesus a peace which is beyond full understanding. I don't have to have a complete answer to the problem of suffering before I can know that peace.

And I have this hope. There is a new world coming because of what God is going to do. And in it there will be no more suffering and no more death, because there will be no more sin. Only what pleases God will be there.

chapter six

Jesus of Nazareth

There is no denying the importance of Jesus of Nazareth in the history of the world and in the lives of at least a thousand million people living today who call him Lord, Saviour, and Son of God. The influential *Time* magazine described him as 'the most persistent symbol of purity, selflessness and brotherly love in the history of western man'.

Jesus has walked through the last two thousand years of history, of changing empires, governments, political systems and philosophies, and has remained a dominant and challenging, yet mysterious, presence.

Fitting the formula

Many writers have tried to face the question 'Who is Jesus?' and to capture his significance for each generation. He has been critically examined as no other, and yet has survived as more challenging than many would have thought possible. The title of one chapter in a book called *Jesus* by Albert Schweitzer puts it well – 'Jesus: The Man who Fits no Formula'. Our vocabulary does not seem adequate to come to grips with the tremendous mystery that is Jesus. Many have presented a Jesus who, in Schweitzer's words, 'was too small because we had forced him into conformity with our human standards and human psychology'.

The historian W. E. H. Lecky, in his book *History of European Morals*, has this to say about Jesus:

'The character of Jesus has not only been the highest pattern of virtue, but the strongest incentive to its practice, and has exerted so deep an influence that it may be truly said that the simple record of three short years of active life has done more to regenerate and soften mankind than all the discussions of philosophers and all the exhortations of moralists.'

In Leningrad, Soviet Russia, the Museum of History of Religion (the Museum of Atheism) has large displays devoted to the abuses of organized religion and its supposed incompatibility with the modern, scientific world. But in the whole building there is nothing about Jesus Christ, no ridicule of him, not one attack on him.

But in the other art museums of Leningrad there are many paintings of Jesus Christ. So even in this professedly atheistic state, Jesus Christ is highly respected.

What do you know of Jesus?

Napoleon Bonaparte said,

'I know men, and I tell you that Jesus Christ is no mere man. Between him and every other person in the world there is no possible term of comparison. Alexander, Caesar, Charlemagne and I founded empires, but on what did we rest the creation of our genius? Upon force. Jesus Christ founded his empire upon love and at this hour millions of men would die for him.'

Jesus' whole life spoke of humility, yet he spoke with such authority. He was known as a man of compassion, and the weakest in society felt safe with him; yet he was a man of strength. He had a great sense of humour, yet people quaked before his anger.

Jesus is unique. His uniqueness lies not just in his mind, ability or power, but in the fact that he is and always has been what God has to say to all people. In Jesus we see what God is like. In Jesus we see what we might become.

Humility and authority, compassion and strength. Unique.

50

Mahatma Gandhi and Dostoevsky are two among thousands, from every race and culture, who have looked at the life of Jesus and said, 'That is how human life ought to be lived.'

History is full of people who have claimed that they have come from God, or that they were gods. Each of them has a right to be heard and considered. But how do we decide whether any of them is justified in his or her claims? Two tests are *reason* and *history*. Reason, because we have it. History, because we live in it.

The man you thought you knew

He was born in an obscure village, the child of a peasant woman. He grew up in another obscure village where he worked in a carpenter's shop until he was thirty. He never wrote a book. He never held an office. He never had a family, or owned a house. He never went to college. He never visited a big city. He never travelled more than two hundred miles from the place where he was born. He did none of those things one usually associated with greatness. He had no credentials but himself.

He was only thirty-three when the tide of public opinion turned against him. His friends ran away. One of them denied him. He was turned over to his enemies and went through the mockery of a trial. He was nailed to a cross between two thieves. While dying, his executioners gambled for his clothing, the only property he had on earth. When he was dead, he was laid in a borrowed grave through the pity of a friend.

Nineteen centuries have come and gone, and today he is the central figure of the human race and the leader of mankind's progress. All the armies that have ever marched, all the navies that ever sailed, all the parliaments that ever sat, all the kings that ever reigned put together have not affected the life on earth of mankind as powerfully as that one solitary life.

Author unknown

Don't force the facts

Reason suggests that if anyone actually did come from God, the least God could do would be to support the messenger's claim by announcing his arrival in advance, and providing some data about him, just as car manufacturers tell the public when to expect a new model and what its features will be. We could then judge the validity of the agent's claims by the extent to which he fitted the data. Otherwise there would be nothing to prevent any imposter from saying 'I come from God' or 'An angel appeared to me in the desert and gave me this message.'

In the writings of the Old Testament, probably completed about four hundred years before Jesus Christ came, there are 322 different prophecies about the 'saviour', who was

thought to be the 'messiah' or chosen one. These prophecies predict his birthplace, his virgin birth, the visitors at his birth, and his mission, to mention just a few of them.

Have these prophecies been historically fulfilled yet? There is no need to force the facts or the prophecies to make them match. They fit each other like a smooth-fitting key in a lock.

Don't hold your breath

According to one mathematician, using the law of compound probability, the chance of these prophecies being fulfilled in one man is represented by a fraction whose numerator is one and the denominator 84 followed by one hundred ciphers. This looks like this:

$$\frac{1}{\substack{840,000,000,000,000,000,000,000,000,000,\\000,000,000,000,000,000,000,000,000,000,\\000,000,000,000,000,000,000,000,000,000,\\000,000,000,000}}$$

A. T. Pierson, *God's Living Oracles*, quoted in Herbert Lockyer, *All the Messianic Prophecies of the Bible*, Zondervan, 1973.

In other words, it doesn't happen every day! History confirms that these 322 prophecies were fulfilled in Jesus Christ.

There'll never be another

Jesus brought to us a new understanding of God – God as Father. He used the most intimate word for 'Father', a word the Jews never used in speaking to God.

But, said Jesus, to experience God as Father, we need to be 'born again' into his family. This is what he told Nicodemus, a leading theologian of his day, explaining to him the necessity of allowing God to remake us from within. To a prostitute, Jesus spoke of being made clean by 'living water', and so beginning to live a new life from now on. That woman was so changed by the teaching of Jesus that she went and brought everybody from her town out to hear him.

The great scourge in Jesus' day was leprosy. It could not be cured, and was highly infectious, so those with leprosy were outcasts from the rest of society. But Jesus not only spoke to them. He did the unthinkable – he touched them. Jesus' compassion reached out to those whom society had rejected.

Jesus always saw people not as 'cases', but as individuals with problems and pains. He saw not just the symptoms of their diseases, but each man or woman as a person for whom he really cared.

> **Jesus always saw people not as 'cases', but as individuals with problems and pains.**

What Jesus taught

Great teachers always point beyond themselves in their teaching. Books written about Buddha, Moses, Mohammed, Plato, Marx, Einstein, regard their philosophy as the key. They would say, 'Don't look at me; look at my teaching. I am not important, my teaching is.'

But with Jesus it is very different. Whereas many teachers past and present have said 'I'm not too sure, but I think this', Jesus made the amazing claim, 'I am the way and the truth and the life. No-one comes to the Father except through me' (*John 14:6*).

He also said, 'Follow me.' He did not bring us a philosophy to discuss or to debate. He brought us himself as the way back to God.

Christianity is accepting the friendship of Jesus and following him. Our obedience to his teaching follows our acceptance of his friendship. The vital issue is not just what we think or believe about Jesus' teaching, but what we do about Jesus.

Who are you?

Jesus used a variety of sayings to describe himself:

- I am the bread of life (*John 6:35*).
- I am the vine; you are the branches. If a man remains in me and I in him, he will bear much fruit; apart from me you can do nothing (*John 15:5*).
- I am the good shepherd. The good shepherd lays down his life for the sheep (*John 10:14*).
- I am the gate, whoever enters through me will be saved (*John 10:9*).
- I am the way and the truth and the life. No-one comes to the Father except through me (*John 14:16*).
- I am the light of the world. Whoever follows me will never walk in darkness, but will have the light of life (*John 8:12*).
- I am the resurrection and the life. He who believes in me will live, even though he dies; and whoever lives and believes in me will never die (*John 11:25–26*).
- I am the Alpha and the Omega, the First and the Last, the beginning and the end (*Revelation 22:13*).

chapter seven

Cross-examination

On a Friday afternoon in April, about AD 30, Jesus of Nazareth was executed by the Roman Empire as a political criminal and freedom fighter on a hill near the city of Jerusalem, Israel.

The night before, Jesus had been praying in Gethsemane, an olive grove east of Jerusalem, with some of his disciples. Suddenly, a crowd of soldiers and religious officials came to the grove carrying torches, lanterns and weapons to arrest Jesus.

His disciples ran off in terror. What had Jesus done wrong? Jesus, the most loving man known in the history of the world, had been arrested. But why?

Religious questions

At last they had him. The religious authorities had been threatened by Jesus and what he had been doing right from the start. Many hundreds, maybe thousands, of people had become his followers in just three years. He had regularly spoken out against the way that the religious leaders conducted themselves. Obviously they couldn't handle Jesus and his new teachings for much longer so something had to be done to silence him. Their plot to capture him had succeeded.

So Jesus was led to the house of Caiaphas, the High Priest, where the Council (the Sanhedrin) was sitting for a special night trial to judge him. It was obvious from the start that Caiaphas and the Council had decided upon the death of Jesus before the trial took place.

//
The most loving man known in the history of the world had been arrested. Why?
//

They queried his teaching to try to catch him out. They wanted to know if he had been preaching secretly or telling the people heresies about God. That would be punishable by death. But no, there was nothing secret about anything he had done. Everyone had heard him, because he had preached in public.

'I have spoken openly to the world. I always taught in synagogues or at the temple, where all the Jews come together. I said nothing in secret. Why question me? Ask those who heard me. Surely they know what I said' (*John 18:20–21*).

Failing to convict him by his own testimony, the Council tried to do so using false witnesses. But this line of attack failed as well. The prosecution witnesses could not agree with each other. At least one of them was lying. The trial was brought to a standstill.

The High Priest then took an extreme step that would force a verdict. Caiaphas asked Jesus: 'Are you the Christ, the Son of the Blessed One?'

Jesus answered: 'I am' (*Mark 14:61–62*).

Then he added: 'I say to all of you: In the future you will see the Son of Man sitting at the right hand of the Mighty One and coming on the clouds of heaven' (*Matthew 26:64*).

Jesus had forced the High Priest to make a decision. Only two possibilities were open to him. Either he had to accept Jesus' claim to be God and believe him, or he had to reject it with the conviction that he had heard an appalling blasphemy.

The High Priest's decision was unequivocal. For him, Jesus' confession that he was the Son of God and that he would sit at God's right hand was a shocking, blasphemous presumption. 'They all condemned him as worthy of death' (*Mark 14:64*).

Immediately a painful scene followed, barely believable in front of a supreme judicial authority. 'Then some began to spit at him;

"

Either he had to accept Jesus' claim to be God and believe him or he had to reject it.

"

they blindfolded him, struck him with their fists, and said "Prophesy!" And the guards took him and beat him' (*Mark 14:65*).

Trial before Pilate

The Romans were the occupying power in Israel and had stripped the Jews of any jurisdiction in cases involving capital offences. So the Jews had no right to carry out a death sentence without the backing of the Roman authorities.

The religious trial of Jesus Christ was over. Now began a political trial to authorize his execution. Thus Jesus was taken to Pilate, the highest-ranking Roman official in the country. The second trial began.

The Council had condemned Jesus for blasphemy, a charge which, according to Jewish law, was punishable by death. But no Roman judge could sentence a Jew to death for a violation of Jewish religious laws.

In full knowledge of this, the Council brought Jesus' case before the Romans under a different guise. How could a Roman court be persuaded to condemn him to death? Jesus would be made out to be a political agitator who threatened the stability of the country.

It was now early on Friday morning. 'Then the whole assembly rose and led him off to Pilate. And they began to accuse him, saying, "We have found this man subverting our nation. He opposes payment of taxes to Caesar and claims to be Christ, a king"' (*Luke 23:1–2*).

They brought three charges against Jesus in order to force Pilate to hear the case. There was no mention of blasphemy. The first and major charge was now sedition. Jesus was unpatriotic, he was a political agitator. He was anti-Caesar, anti-Roman and a danger to the state. In short, he was a deceiver who had been inducing people to follow a direction other than that dictated by Rome.

Jesus and the poll tax

That was the first charge. Secondly they

> **We have found this man subverting our nation.**

claimed he had urged the people not to pay taxes to Caesar. And thirdly, they asserted that he had set himself up as a rival to Pilate.

He was a political threat, a freedom fighter and a 'king'. These were the Council's charges.

One charge in particular worried Pilate. *Was* this prisoner before him a King? Was he a real threat to Pilate's authority? Pilate summoned Jesus privately and asked him, 'Are you the king of the Jews?' (*John 18:33*).

Jesus replied: 'My kingdom is not of this world. If it were, my servants would fight to prevent my arrest ... my kingdom is from another place' (*John 18:36*).

Jesus made a distinction between political and religious kingship. Political kingship, which was the only interest Pilate had in the case, Jesus rejected. Religious kingship, which meant that he was divine, Jesus admitted.

Pilate went to the Jews and reported, 'I find no basis for a charge against him' (*John 18:38*).

Pilate was now confused. As far as he could see, Jesus did not deserve to die. And yet the Council were out for his blood. So he tried to create a basis for an acquittal of Jesus. For this he needed the help of Herod Antipas, tetrarch of Galilee. Thus Jesus was sent to Herod.

Herod did Pilate the expected favour by giving Jesus an audience. But he conducted it in his own way. He asked Jesus many questions and hoped to see him work a miracle. But Jesus remained silent throughout.

Herod began to get irritated. His pride had been insulted. 'Then Herod and his soldiers ridiculed and mocked him. Dressing him in an elegant robe, they sent him back to Pilate' (*Luke 23:11*).

A second sitting before Pilate

When Jesus arrived back again, Pilate was obliged to sum up the case before the Council. 'I have examined him in your presence and

have found no basis for your charges against him. Neither has Herod, for he sent him back to us; as you can see, he has done nothing to deserve death. Therefore, I will punish him and then release him' (*Luke 23:14–16*).

Was ever a more illogical 'therefore' uttered? Imagine a scene in a modern court of law today. The person in question is in the dock, all the evidence is given. The jury retires and considers the evidence and returns with a 'not guilty' verdict. The prisoner smiles, waves to his family and friends in the court; in turn they wave congratulations. The judge then stands and tells the court, 'This man has been tried and the jury declares him innocent. I have therefore decided to sentence him to five years' hard labour.'

The penalty of death on the cross was considered so horrible and dishonourable that it could be inflicted only on non-Romans.

Blood

Unbelievable injustice! Yet it happened to Jesus.

Pilate tried to strike a balance between satisfying the Sanhedrin and salving his own conscience. But Pilate was wrong in thinking that the drawing of blood would calm their passions and melt them to pity. If guilty, Pilate should have condemned him to death. If innocent, he should have released him.

So Jesus was scourged, whipped by Roman soldiers. Jesus had to submit to a punishment so gruesome that it alone could have caused his death.

Josephus, a Jewish historian at the time, described how, as a guerrilla commander in Galilee, he himself had once ordered the scourging of some of his countrymen: '. . . a scourging so lacerating that their entrails were laid bare'.

The Jewish War, II.

Another historian recorded that 'some died at once from the terrible wounds during the scourging, while others lay sick for a long time, despairing of recovery'.

Philo, in Flaccus.

The Roman guards took Jesus away, leading him to a pillar in the punishment block. The prescribed whipping was about to begin. His hands were tied together with rope and they were fastened up above him so that his feet barely touched the ground. The duty centurion took up the whip – a leather handle binding together several thongs, with pieces of bone or metal embedded. After the first three or four lashes his back would have been a mass of blood and ripped skin. As the metal and bone tore at the skin of his back, chunks of flesh would have flown off.

Eventually, they cut Jesus down so that he would have collapsed at the foot of the pillar, lying in his own blood. Not content with the horror of the whipping alone, the soldiers picked him up and began to mock him. They put a cloak around him and pushed a 'crown' of thorns down on to his head. 'So you're the King of the Jews!' they laughed.

The Barabbas factor

Meanwhile the Council were furious with Pilate for letting Jesus go. It just so happened that Pilate had a custom of releasing one prisoner during the Jewish festival known as Passover. He suggested that the people choose the one they wanted to be released.

The man the Jews wanted was named Barabbas. He had been thrown into prison with several others who had been involved in an uprising and who had committed murder in its cause. Pilate proposed Jesus as his candidate for the Passover amnesty.

But Pilate underestimated his opponents' tactics. The Jewish authorities increased their support of Barabbas and stirred up the city mob.

So Pilate soon found himself facing a mass of screaming people who yelled in organized chorus, 'Crucify him!' (*Mark 15:13*).

Eventually Pilate, wanting to satisfy the crowd, yielded to the Council's pressure. He had Barabbas released and handed Jesus over to be crucified as a political prisoner.

Pilate then 'took water and washed his hands in front of the crowd. "I am innocent of this man's blood," he said. "It is your responsibility!"' (*Matthew 27:24*).

Crucify him!

Nailing the Truth

Pilate's cowardice resulted in death for Jesus, a death by one of the crudest methods of execution ever devised by humans for humans.

With the Romans, the penalty of death on the cross was considered so horrible and dishonourable that it could be inflicted only on non-Romans.

Cicero wrote: 'A hangman, a covered head,

Pro Rabiro 16.

and the very word "cross" should remain far not only from the body of Roman citizens, but also from their thoughts, their eyes, their ears.'

So they took off his cloak, put his own clothes on him, placed the upright beam on the cross on his back and led him out. At one point along the route, Jesus fell down. Think about what had happened. Jesus had been awake for the last thirty-six hours. He had been submitted to six different hearings. He had been whipped and mocked and had been convicted of a crime he did not commit. He now lay in the road with a beam on his blood-covered back.

Jesus was so exhausted he could barely keep going. The soldiers grabbed a bystander from the crowd, Simon of Cyrene, and made him carry the beam.

Finally, they all arrived at the place assigned for the crucifixion – Golgotha, which means 'Place of the Skull'.

> **He was whipped, mocked, stripped, nailed . . . the final stage of his slow, painful death had begun.**

The beam was taken from Simon of Cyrene and was fastened against another beam to make a cross. Jesus was stripped and laid on the cross. His hands and feet were tied fast. Then one of the soldiers took some nails, six inches of rough iron, and drove them into his hands and through his feet.

Jesus was offered a drugged drink to deaden the pain, but he refused it. A hole had already been dug, and several soldiers raised the cross with Jesus on it and thrust it in the hole. With that jolt pain would have surged through his body, nerves and muscle fibre still ripping where the nails had punctured his limbs. The final stage of his slow and painful death had begun.

An inscription was placed on the top of the cross, stating the reason for the condemnation: 'Jesus of Nazareth, the King of the Jews.'

Words at the cross

While Jesus was hanging on the cross, people standing there hurled insults at him. Other mockers called out for him to come down from the cross to demonstrate his miraculous powers to them.

Others responded totally differently. They realized that Jesus was indeed who he claimed to be. A criminal, crucified next to him, asked him in his last hours of life for help. 'Jesus, remember me when you come into your kingdom,' he said. The truth of Jesus' identity also dawned on the centurion on duty: 'Surely this man was the Son of God,' he exclaimed.

In spite of the agony of the crucifixion and the mockery and cynicism of those around him, Jesus continued to offer forgiveness, life and hope. 'Father, forgive them, for they do not know what they are doing' (*Luke 23:34*).

The greatest agony

But this was nothing compared to the spiritual agony that Jesus was suffering. As he hung there, Jesus was taking on himself the weight and heaviness of all the sin and all the guilt in the whole world. *Everything* that has ever been done wrong, *everything* you and I have ever done wrong, was being put on him.

As the sky blackened with thunder clouds, Jesus shouted out with a piercing cry: 'My God, my God, why have you forsaken me?' (*Matthew 27:46*).

Jesus was repeating the words of Psalm 22, a prophecy referring to himself, written hundreds of years before in the Old Testament of the Bible. The awful reality of Jesus' agony was being exposed. By taking on to himself the sins of the world he had to suffer the most awful consequence: rejection by God himself. All the desolating effects of sin were fully loaded on to Jesus – a sense of dark abandonment, utter loneliness and sheer separation from God. To deal with sin he experienced the hell of abandonment. That is *total* loneliness.

Then Jesus shouted out, 'It is finished.'
It is accomplished. It is fulfilled. It is done. Sin had been dealt with.

Finished.

65

Finally, after six hours on the cross, Jesus said, 'Father, into your hands I commit my spirit' (*Luke 23:46*).

The words were shouted, not spoken in an exhausted whisper, as when people breathe their last. Jesus had already said that no-one would take away his life, but that he would lay it down himself.

Death did not tap on his shoulder, summoning Jesus to depart. He went out to meet death!

So Jesus died.

chapter eight

Cross-purposes

Why did he let himself get killed?

The first followers of Jesus Christ met with opposition and many challenges. The main challenge was, 'Why, if Jesus was the promised Messiah, did he die?'

Among the enemies of Jesus were the Pharisees. There were about 6,000 of them in Jerusalem during his time. They had a tremendous zeal for the law of Moses and a passion for doing right. They assumed they could lead a perfect lifestyle by following some 613 commandments. The great mistake they made was to imagine that they could succeed!

The Pharisees rejected Jesus because they considered him outrageously lax in his attitude to the law of Moses and far too dismissive of their elaborations of it. These proud men could not accept the fact that a carpenter from Nazareth (of all places) could possibly be the chosen person through whom God was rescuing the world.

Another group of opponents were the Sadducees from whom the high priests were drawn. They were the spiritual aristocrats of their day. Jesus was totally unacceptable to them because he was a commoner. For the Pharisees and Sadducees, the true Christ would immediately liberate the nation from bondage to a foreign power. So a crucified Jesus seemed like a joke!

- Why did he die?
- What did his death achieve?

Those two questions about the death of Jesus are still basic.

A crucified Jesus seemed like a joke!

The political journalist – surface reasons

The first and obvious reason for Jesus' death was of course that some of his contemporaries did not like him. Telling religious teachers that they were lost or that they should turn away from their sins was not popular. Their reaction was something like, 'How dare he come into our world disturbing, interrupting and interfering! And anyway, who does this ignorant person think he is?' So they decided his career must be brought to an end.

The state also had its say in the death of Jesus. Jesus acknowledged Caesar and the rights of the state and made reference to our duties to it. But he set limits to the claims of the state. It cannot demand the total obedience that

belongs only to God. This has been made clear in every period of history from Nebuchadnezzar and Augustus to Hitler and Stalin.

The reason the state, represented by Pilate, agreed without firm protest to the condemnation of Jesus was that he posed a political threat. Jesus had spoken about his kingdom, a different one from the Roman Empire. Jesus had said that he was a king too, so where did that leave Herod? But Jesus was never really a political threat to the Empire. He said, 'My kingdom is not of this world.'

Even so, Jesus did challenge any idea of the state that claimed people's total allegiance, especially the idea that the Emperor represents God! When Pilate and Jesus met, what they each stood for was in conflict. A momentous issue was at stake – Christ or Caesar.

The trial of Jesus was not completely undemocratic, even though it was conducted in

... a rescue act, reaching down to the deepest point of our need.

an undemocratic fashion. The people also had their say. When Pilate offered to release Jesus at the Passover, a crowd spurred on by rabble-rousers called for the release of Barabbas, a notorious revolutionary, and shouted for the crucifixion of Jesus.

Different classes of people were involved in sending Jesus to his death because:
- The teaching of Jesus had threatened the religious authorities.
- The kingdom of Jesus had threatened the state.
- The morality of Jesus had threatened the people.

Jesus demanded a decision. A choice. People could either repent and ask for forgiveness, as some did, or they could reject him and shout 'Crucify him!'

We still have that choice.

Today we still have that choice. We must decide too. But that is sometimes too difficult for us. Although we may think that we are good, a truly 'good' man makes us feel uncomfortable.

Behind the scenes – the deeper reasons

Death did not take Jesus by surprise. His crucifixion was no unforeseen accident. Many times throughout his three years of public teaching, Jesus made reference to his death. He knew that it had to happen, that it was inevitable. He knew that God's purpose would be fulfilled through people, even through their wrong motives. I am amazed, but not surprised, by the way that God's purpose was accomplished through events which he can hardly be said to have directly caused. God did not cause Caiaphas to seek the death of Jesus, nor Judas to betray him, nor Pilate to condemn him. But God took their evil choices and wove them into his purpose.

This was a key point in the teaching of the first disciples. They answered the question

'Why did Jesus die?' on two levels. First, without any embarrassment they laid the responsibility and guilt on the people themselves. But they also saw God's plan in it all. 'This man was handed over to you by God's set purpose and foreknowledge; and you, with the help of wicked men, put him to death by nailing him to the cross' (*Acts 2:23*).

Therefore the death of Jesus was the fulfilment of God's purpose. Jesus went with it all because there was no other way by which the sins of the world could be dealt with.

What did his death achieve?

In the cross we see the real horror of sin. Sin is anti-God and causes him moral outrage and pain. So God has to deal with sin. And the death of his Son, Jesus, on the cross is what it cost God to deal with it.

Imagine that you and everyone you know are trapped in a room with me. I will never let any of you leave. You can't escape, because I am stronger than all of you put together, and I have locked all the exits. You are trapped. No matter what you try to do, you just can't get out. You could escape only if someone outside the room, who is stronger than me, broke down the door and rescued you.

That's a bit like what God has done for us. To sum it up in one word, it is 'rescue'. God's action in the cross is a rescue act, reaching down to the deepest point of our need.

" . . . rescued. "

The word the Bible uses for 'rescue' is 'redeem'. The word for rescuer is redeemer. A redeemer is a great benefactor who frees slaves by actually paying a ransom price for them. This is what Jesus Christ has done for mankind through the cross. He has set us free from the slavery of sin by breaking sin's power over us through his life-saving death.

Blood the only way

The price of redemption was infinitely costly. In Christ 'we have redemption through his blood' (*Ephesians 1:7*).

The word 'blood' is a kind of shorthand for a 'life laid down in death'. Why was it necessary that the blood of Christ should be shed? Because *he* accepted the death *we* deserved to die for our sins. And only *his* blood would do, because only he, as the one person who never sinned, could satisfy God's outraged justice. As the hymn puts it:

> 'There was no other good enough
> To pay the price of sin;
> He only could unlock the gate
> Of heaven and let us in.'

It is only when God himself deals with the sin that affronts him that forgiveness can be experienced, because we cannot live with God so long as our guilt is still there. We cannot simply shrug off our guilt either, because God's anger against our sins really matters. We cannot take lightly what he takes so seriously.

In the cross, the strength of God's love more than matches the power of his anger. But not at the expense of his justice – for in Jesus Christ God himself satisfied his righteous demand that sin be punished once and for all. As Peter the apostle put it: 'Christ died for sins once and for all, a good man on behalf of sinners, in order to lead you to God' (*1 Peter 3:18, Good News Bible*).

The cross is the movement of God towards the people he loves – both you and me. The cross unites separated parties. The Bible's word for this is 'reconciliation'. The cross of Jesus enabled God and mankind to meet on new terms. Sin had caused an estrangement. But now the cause of it – sin – has been removed. Through the cross an entirely new relationship comes about between us and God. We are no longer enemies but friends.

In all this God took the initiative, not us. We are at the receiving end. We could not have reconciled ourselves to God. But now, through the one mediator, Jesus Christ, we can enter

There need no longer be feelings of hostility towards ourselves.

into a relationship with God.

The good news is that we can meet with God through the cross of Jesus Christ. There need no longer be feelings of hostility towards ourselves, others and God. This leads us into a new freedom. We don't have to live under a sense of condemnation, failure and frustration.

The great agony . . .

The word 'crucifixion' means to 'fasten to a cross'. It dates back to 600 BC and was abolished by the Emperor Constantine in the fifth century AD. It is a symbol of the cruellest and the most painful death that has ever been invented by man.

Jesus Christ regarded his death as absolutely central to everything he did. No other death has raised a fraction of interest or concern by comparison.

And of all the things Jesus could have asked us to remember, number one was his death.

Jesus was stripped, tied to a post and flogged (*Matthew 27:26–31*). His body would have become raw, inflamed and bleeding. With a crown of thorns on his head and a beam tied to his back, he was led to Golgotha, where he was nailed to a cross.

. . . the great achievement

Jesus died that he might bring us to God. That's to say, the purpose of the death of Jesus was not first and foremost to show us something, or to teach us something, but to *do* something for us. The cross was an achievement because it brings us *to* God, so that our sins no longer separate us *from* God.

By dying, Jesus purchased for us forgiveness. One of the New Testament words is 'justify', which means 'declare innocent'. Because Jesus died for our guilt, it is now possible for us to be declared innocent.

73

And there's more. When we experience reconciliation we are given the privilege of being in God's family. Standing within this new relationship and enjoying this new liberty, we can begin to become the people God meant us to be. Out of this new relationship which the cross brings about, moral progress and transformation come.

The full treatment

When God forgives us for Christ's sake he accepts us as we are. So we don't have to pretend any more. We can now face ourselves and what we have done without being driven to despair. For God 'declares the guilty to be innocent' (*Romans 4:5*) – declares us righteous in his sight on the basis of the once-for-all death of Christ for us. When we grasp this wonderful truth, the healing of all our hurts begins. I can accept myself because God has accepted me.

C. S. Lewis described the Christian life as 'going in for the full treatment'. Jesus promised that, after he returned to heaven, God would send the Holy Spirit to live within every person who is reconciled to God. Turning from our sins and asking for Christ's forgiveness gives us the privilege of receiving his Holy Spirit.

The Holy Spirit is a bit like an interpreter. He reveals Jesus to us, illuminating his teaching and applying the significance of his death on the cross to our lives. He helps us to know God intimately and gives us direction in life.

But he is more than an interpreter. For he brings Jesus into our lives as the one who saves us and becomes our Lord and Friend. For if the Holy Spirit lives in us, so does Jesus.

We cannot fully understand the cross. It has depths to it that we cannot plumb – depths of love and mercy that we shall never exhaust. But this we can know: Jesus died for sinners, and *this* sinner needs to respond to such amazing love.

> **When we grasp this, the healing of all our hurts begins.**

chapter nine

What happened at God's funeral

The burial of Jesus

When Jesus was crucified, he died at about 3 o'clock on the afternoon that we now celebrate as Good Friday. It was only a few hours before the sabbath began – a holy day on which no work could be done. So Joseph of Arimathea, an influential member of the Jewish Council who was a follower of Jesus, got permission from Pilate to take away Jesus' body. He took it down from the cross, wrapped it in linen cloth and placed it in an empty tomb cut into the rock in a garden near to the crucifixion site. Several close friends, including Jesus' mother and Mary Magdalene, saw where Jesus' body was laid, because after the Sabbath they intended to anoint his body with spices and perfumes as was the custom. Before leaving, they rolled a large stone over the tomb entrance. Then they went home.

Meanwhile, some of the religious authorities went to Pilate to ask for the tomb to be guarded. They were worried that the disciples of Jesus would steal the body and spread a story that he had risen from the dead. So Pilate set a guard at the burial site and had a Roman seal put on the stone that blocked the tomb entrance. Breaking a Roman seal without permission meant execution!

After the sabbath, at dawn on Sunday, Mary Magdalene and a few other women went to the tomb with prepared spices and perfumes to

> **He died at about 3 o'clock on the afternoon that we now celebrate as Good Friday.**

anoint Jesus' body. When the women got there they found that the stone had been rolled away. Nearby stood an angel who told them that Jesus had been raised from the dead! He was alive! 'Now go and tell the disciples,' he said.

As soon as they heard about it, two of the disciples, Peter and John, ran down to the garden – to find the tomb empty, with only the folded graveclothes left inside. They went away confused.

Mary Magdalene returned to the tomb in tears. Kneeling on the ground, she noticed someone nearby. She asked, 'Where have you put him?'

The man simply replied, 'Mary.'

There was only one man who said it quite like that. She knew it was Jesus. 'Jesus! You're alive!' she thought. He told her to tell the disciples that he was actually alive.

This was the first appearance of Jesus after he had risen from the dead. He went on to make many other appearances to many other people as recorded in the New Testament of the Bible.

The resurrection of Jesus Christ from the dead is the foundation of Christianity. If he did not rise from the dead, then there is no truth in Christianity. It does not have anything to stand on. Christianity as a religion is unique because it is based on the death and resurrection of its founder. So either it is the biggest hoax in the history of the world or it is true. If it is true, it should stand the test. What is the evidence for the resurrection?

Before we even consider what evidence there is for the resurrection of Jesus Christ, we must look at two suggestions which deny that the resurrection ever happened.

> **If Jesus did not rise from the dead, there is no truth in Christianity.**

All in the mind?

It has been said that the disciples were deluded. They expected him to rise from the dead and they then imagined that this had happened. The whole idea of the resurrection is wish fulfilment. 'It's all in the mind.'

But the disciples didn't expect Jesus to rise from the dead. The truth is the exact opposite. In every case when Jesus appears to them after his death, the visits are unexpected and at first unaccepted. The disciples didn't convince themselves. It was Jesus who had to convince them.

To say that all the disciples were deluded also contradicts principles to which psychologists say delusions conform. Only certain types of people have them. Delusions are very individualistic and extremely subjective. It is therefore extremely unlikely that two people would have the same hallucination at the same time. Delusions are never corporate like this.

If the disciples were deluded, declaring to everyone that Jesus had risen from the dead, then all the Jewish leaders and Roman authorities had to do was to produce the body of Jesus. This they could not do, for the tomb was empty and they did not have the body.

Did he really die?

Others have suggested that Jesus didn't actually die on the cross. They claim that Jesus just fainted on the cross and that in the coolness of the garden tomb he recovered consciousness. They suggest that (after suffering extreme torture) he somehow wriggled out of the graveclothes (remembering to fold them, of course!), pushed the stone aside, and overpowered the Roman sentry guards! Thus his post-crucifixion appearances are 'explained' without the miracle of resurrection.

Contrary to this, the Bible clearly states that when Jesus was taken down from the cross, the Roman guards pierced his side with a spear to make sure that he was dead.

Delusions are never corporate like this.

So what is the evidence that he rose again?

The empty tomb

The first piece of evidence that Jesus rose from the dead is that the guarded tomb where he was buried was empty after three days. The grave-clothes were found neatly folded where Jesus once lay. Either the body was stolen or he did actually rise from the dead.

It is highly unlikely that the followers of Jesus would have stolen his body. It is clear from the Bible that they were frightened and that they were not expecting Jesus to rise from the dead. So why steal the body? Why not just leave it there, quietly and reverently? In any case, even if they had tried to steal it, they would have had to get past the Roman guards.

What about the religious authorities? They couldn't have stolen the body. If they had, as soon as the disciples started saying that Jesus was alive, all they had to do was to produce his dead body to put an end to the rumours. This did not happen.

The body wasn't stolen. The tomb was empty. Could he really have risen?

The appearances

After his death, Jesus appeared alive on twelve separate occasions to at least 550 different people. A court of law today would find this very impressive because of the number of witnesses involved.

One of the disciples, Thomas, wanted absolute physical proof that Jesus was alive by actually touching his wounded scars. Even he was convinced, following a personal encounter with the risen Christ.

. . . proof, absolute . . .

The change in the disciples

Something phenomenal happened to the disciples of Jesus. Following his death they went into hiding, frightened of the authorities. Within forty days they began publicly declaring that Jesus was alive. Many of them were martyred for being Christians. This did not deter the other disciples.

It is true that some people will die for something they sincerely think is true. But if the disciples had fabricated the story of the resurrection, they would hardly have died for it. The disciples' lives and attitudes were turned upside down after the death of Jesus, and it is hard to be convinced that their motivation was anything other than what they claimed: Jesus had risen.

'Perhaps the transformation of the disciples of Jesus is the greatest evidence of all in favour of the Resurrection,' wrote John Stott.

Christians and the church today

An unbroken succession of millions throughout every century can witness that their lives have been revolutionized by the living Jesus Christ. Rich and poor, educated and uneducated, people of different cultures and nationalities, all unite in their experience of having met Jesus Christ.

The existence of the Christian church is a historical fact that demands an explanation. How did it grow so quickly and have such an influence, even capturing the Roman Empire?

An often overlooked piece of evidence for the resurrection of Jesus Christ is the change of the day of regular weekly worship from the Jewish Sabbath (Saturday) to Sunday, the day of the resurrection. Could anything be more fixed in religious tradition than the custom of keeping the seventh day as a special day for worship, as practised in Judaism? Hardly. Yet, from the very beginning, we see Christians

> **The existence of the Christian church is a historical fact that demands an explanation.**

C. S. Lewis said: 'A Christian believes in Jesus not because he finds him by laboratory methods, but by actual contact with him. The Christian is something like the electric eel, which knows more about electricity than all the electrical engineers put together.'

Contact

switching away from the Sabbath as their day of worship, and instead worshipping on Sunday.

What can account for that? The resurrection of Jesus Christ: an event so significant that it immediately produced the most profound changes, not only in the moral character of the early believers, but in their habits of life and forms of worship as well.

A former Lord Chief Justice of England, Lord Darling, once said: 'In its favour as a living truth, there exists such overwhelming evidence, positive and negative, factual and circumstantial, that no intelligent jury in the world can fail to bring in a verdict that the resurrection is true.'

Quoted by Michael Green, *The Day Death Died*, IVP, 1982, p. 15.

All this may make it reasonable to believe in the resurrection of Jesus Christ. But it is not just reasonable, but realistic too. The real evidence for the resurrection is Jesus Christ himself.

'The message of the early church was that not only is Jesus Christ alive, but that we can actually meet him for ourselves. After all, the best way of finding out whether someone really exists is not to prove or disprove it, but to meet them.'

Val Grieve, *Your Verdict*, IVP, 1988, p. 95.

We can meet Jesus Christ today and know him as the Son of God (powerful) and yet as a friend (personal). This makes Christianity alive and unique.

So what?

There are three crucial implications of Jesus' rising from the dead. The resurrection shows us that Jesus is the Son of God, that forgiveness is now possible, and that death is not the end.

1. Jesus is the Son of God

When you think about Jesus' life and teaching, he made some staggering claims about himself. He claimed to be the Son of God, able to forgive people's sins and offer them a new life. But

. . . either a fraud or a terribly deluded man.

some people who do not accept his claim to be the Son of God say that he was simply a good teacher or just a good man. But how can he be good if he was misleading them as to his identity? Either he was who he claimed to be or he wasn't. If he wasn't, he certainly couldn't be 'good', because he would be either a fraud or a terribly deluded man. Either way he would not be worth trusting.

But the resurrection of Jesus stops us in our tracks. He doesn't leave us with the option of saying that he was just a great teacher. Having said he would rise from the dead, he did exactly that – something no other great teacher has ever done! By the resurrection, Jesus Christ has shown himself to be no less than what he claimed to be – the Son of God and the Saviour of the world.

2. Forgiveness is now possible

Jesus said that we could be forgiven only by trusting him and what he did on the cross. The only way we know that his death was effective and therefore that forgiveness is possible is that Jesus did in fact rise from the dead. Nothing could assure us more than that. The resurrection assures us that Jesus' death was worthwhile and that it did achieve its goal. His death did indeed pay the price of our sin and gain us access to God.

3. Death is not the end

Because Jesus rose from the dead we know that death is not the end. Death was the final barrier that sin had caused and it was the last barrier that he had to overcome. By rising from the dead, Jesus showed us that he had indeed overcome death. With Jesus as our Lord and God we can look at death and face it confidently when we are joined to him, by faith.

We can look at death and face it confidently . . .

The resurrection of Jesus Christ from the dead authenticates everything that Jesus said here on earth. It authenticates everything he did here on earth. And it tells us that death isn't the end.

Christianity is based both on evidence for the resurrection and on the fact of it. The evidence is there because Jesus really did rise from the dead. It is based on objective, external historical facts and on the subjective, internal, personal experience of Jesus Christ. Because he is alive, he can now be experienced personally when we trust our lives to him.

Vicious hoax or fantastic fact

'I have come to the conclusion that the resurrection of Jesus Christ is either one of the most wicked, vicious, heartless hoaxes ever foisted upon the minds of men, or it is the most fantastic fact of history.'

Josh McDowell, *Evidence that Demands a Verdict* (Here's Life, 1972), p. 179.

chapter ten

The end of the beginning

In this book we have explored the claims of Jesus Christ. We have looked at what Jesus Christ said about himself and what he said about us. He said simply that we are lost in darkness and that he had come to guide us and bring light into our lives. He had come to bring us into a close relationship with God.

We simply cannot remain neutral about Jesus Christ. We have to make a choice. We are on one side or the other. Jesus said, 'He who is not with me is against me' (*Matthew 12:30*). So where do you stand? Are you for Jesus or against him?

Many people seem to think that 'just thinking about it' is an option. Yes, in one sense it is. But because you are not for him and with him you are still against him. The pop group The Alarm sing

> 'The truth is surely the truth
> or the truth is surely a lie
> Get back in your shelter
> if you can't come down off the fence.'

A decision must be made.

There are three options that lie before you. You can say, 'No, I do not want to have anything to do with it,' forget the whole thing, and do nothing else about it. You can say, 'I can't decide yet, but I will seriously look into it more.' Or you can say, 'Yes, I do want to have this relationship with Jesus.'

> **We simply cannot remain neutral.**

Declaration, IRS Records, 1983

Becoming a Christian

The name 'Christian' was first given to those people in Antioch who believed in Jesus Christ and lived by his teaching.

Going to church or trying to live a good life does not make us Christians. For being a Christian means having a relationship with God. In this relationship we soon discover God's constant love, friendship, trustworthiness and peace. And we find we can be ourselves because he accepts us as we are (warts and all). But we don't stop there, because we also see what we may become (more like Jesus) as we continue to get to know him.

So how can I become a Christian?

Admitting

We must realize that we are distanced from God and therefore we don't have a relationship with him. In a nutshell, we have rejected God and have done our own thing. This is the root sin. First of all, then, we need to admit that this is where we are at.

Committing

As we look at what Jesus Christ did on the cross for us we realize that he has dealt with our sin. As we commit our lives to Jesus Christ, we can give him our sin and therefore receive his forgiveness from the past. To begin a relationship with him we must receive his Holy Spirit, whom he gives to live within us.

When we begin a friendship with God we receive his Holy Spirit into our life. In the physical world life is created as soon as conception takes place. In the spiritual world life begins whenever anyone believing in Jesus Christ receives the new life he offers and so is 'born again'. It is God's Holy Spirit entering our lives that makes us a child of God and a member of his family.

We cannot belong to God's family unless his

We need to admit that this is where we are at.

Spirit lives in us. 'If anyone does not have the Spirit of Christ, he does not belong to Christ' (*Romans 8:9*).

This is not just turning over a new leaf or having a moral clean-up. This is a new *life* – God's life entering us.

Submitting

It is one thing to admit that we have sinned and to commit our life to God by receiving his Spirit. It is quite another actually to live it out. Many people call themselves 'Christians' without actually submitting fully to God. We must be prepared to allow God to work in our lives without restricting him.

The Holy Spirit comes into our lives to illuminate his teaching (the Bible), to help us with our communication with God (prayer), and to join us to his whole family (the church), so that we not only believe in him but belong to him.

God wants us to be in fellowship with him through his Son Jesus Christ. He longs for us to have a confident friendship with him. So what will you do? Will you admit to him that you have sinned and commit your life to him? Yes or no?

If you want to say yes, then say these words as a prayer to Jesus, who is the way to God, to begin this relationship with him.

Thank you, Jesus, for dying on the cross.
Thank you, Jesus, that I can come to you now
    because you are alive.
I admit that I have lived my life without you,
    and that I have broken your laws.
I commit myself to you and I ask for your
    forgiveness.
I receive you into my life by your Holy Spirit.
Help me to submit my life to your teaching
    and to your direction from this moment on.
Amen.

How can I be sure?

Whenever a president pardons a convicted

This is not just turning over a new leaf or a moral clean up.

criminal, he has this fact brought to the person's attention! Similarly, if God freely forgives our sins and allows us to enter into a relationship with him, we should expect that he will assure us of the fact.

The assurance of our relationship with God is rather like sitting on a three-legged stool. When all three legs are there, we are secure. If only two legs are there, we are a bit wobbly. And if only one is there, we are likely to fall over!

The three legs of Christian assurance are:
1. The Word of God – the Bible.
2. The work of Christ – what he has done for us.
3. The presence of the Spirit – who lives in us.
All three are needed for us to be stable as Christians.

God's written Word is the Bible. In it God has clearly promised to give eternal life and a relationship with him to those who become Christians. 'The testimony is this: God has given us eternal life, and this life has its source in his Son. Whoever has the Son has this life; whoever does not have the Son of God does not have life.' It is not arrogant or proud to believe this. In fact it would be a sin to doubt this, as 'whoever does not believe God, has made him out to be a liar, because he has not believed what God has said about his Son' (*1 John 5:10–12, Good News Bible*).

The second leg of the stool is what Christ has done for us: his dying on the cross in our place, and his resurrection and victory over death for us. If we have looked at the evidence and become Christians, we can be sure of Christ's work and our relationship with God.

We can be just as sure as I am that I'm married to my wife, Killy. It is not just that I *feel* married. On 23 July 1983 I committed my life to Killy Ann Rees, as she then was, and I know I am now married. In the same way, on 9 February 1975 I committed my life to Jesus Christ

"
This is not the end of the story.
"

as my Saviour and my King. Both were once-and-for-all events.

But this is not the end of the story. The third leg of the stool is the Holy Spirit whom Christians experience in their lives. This is not mere emotion, elated one day and insecure the next. Becoming a Christian, like being married, has begun to alter my character, my priorities in life and my actions. I can see the effect. As a Christian, God's Spirit is changing me from within. As the Bible says, 'Those who are led by God's Spirit are God's sons' (*Romans 8:14, Good News Bible*).

At a very deep level Christians can know that something unique has happened to them. 'God's Spirit joins himself to our Spirit to declare that we are God's children' (*Romans 8:16*). This is far deeper than passing emotion. It is the personal conviction created by the Holy Spirit that we are forgiven, belong to him for ever, and are part of God's family, the church. This conviction grows as we obey the teaching of the Bible and pray for the transforming power of the Spirit in our lives.

'If there is anything to what I say . . . it should be seen in my life.'

Bono, U2, 1982, quoted in
Steve Turner, *Hungry for Heaven*.

The first steps

Jesus Christ's first call to you is to himself. One Christian, Martin Luther, said, 'I do not know the way that I take but well do I know my guide.' I would rather have an experienced guide than a detailed map. A good guide may not inform me how he is going to arrive at the desired destination, but he will give me good directions when needed. Best of all, a guide is a companion on the journey. Jesus offers to guide us like no other.

If you have decided to follow Jesus Christ, you must begin to get to know him. He has been described in the Bible as the good shepherd, so as you get to know him you will be able to hear him and follow his leading.

Begin to depend on the following things:

The Bible

The Bible is a library of sixty-six 'books'. Don't be led to thinking that only some of it is relevant. Jesus declared the Old Testament to be true. The Old Testament is mostly history, the history of how God dealt with his own people. But don't be put off by the word 'history'; it is full of sound and vital advice! The poet Steve Turner wrote in his collection of poems, *Nice and Nasty*,

> 'History repeats itself.
> Has to.
> No-one listens.'

The Old Testament teaches how God guided people in the past and tells us to expect the same God to guide us today.

The New Testament consists of four accounts of the life of Jesus, called 'gospels'. What he said and did is presented from four different perspectives by Matthew, Mark, Luke and John. Then follows the book of Acts, a historical account of how the Christian church started and began to grow. The next twenty-one books are letters written to churches and individuals to guide them over difficulties and misunderstandings. The last book, Revelation, is an encouragement to look beyond the present to the new world that will be brought into being when God's kingdom is fully established.

Reading and studying the Bible, in a modern translation, will increase your knowledge and understanding of God. It will develop and strengthen your character and show you God's purpose.

In an excellent book called *The Fight* (worth

" God does not desire to guide us magically. He wants us to know his mind. "

reading!), John White says, 'God does not desire to guide us magically. He wants us to know his mind. He wants us to grasp his very heart. We need minds so soaked with the content of Scripture [the Bible], so imbued with biblical outlooks and principles, so sensitive to the Holy Spirit's prompting that we will know instinctively the upright step to take in any circumstance, small or great ... through the study of [Scripture] you may become acquainted with the ways and thoughts of God.'

John White, *The Fight*, IVP, 1977, p.157

Prayer

Jesus longs for us to have a confident friendship with him. The key to this is prayer. The twelve disciples of Jesus asked him how to pray and Jesus said,

> 'This is how you should pray:
>   Our Father in heaven,
> hallowed be your name,
> your kingdom come,
> your will be done,
>   on earth as it is in heaven.
> Give us today our daily bread.
> Forgive us our debts,
>   as we also have forgiven our debtors.
> And lead us not into temptation,
> but deliver us from the evil one.'
>   (*Matthew 6:9–13*)

We will know instinctively the upright step to take in any circumstance.

The first three statements of this prayer are all concerned with God's glory. It is always good to start any prayer time by acknowledging who God is and making the doing of his will foremost in your desires. As you do this you may become conscious of sinning since you last spoke to him. If so, confess the sin to him and receive his forgiveness and cleansing.

'If we confess our sins, he is faithful and just and will forgive us our sins and purify us from all unrighteousness' (*1 John 1:9*).

Tell God what has happened, acknowledge that you may have hurt him, someone else or even yourself – and receive forgiveness.

Jesus then said, 'Give us today our daily bread.' Pray for God's goodness to be shown in your basic daily needs for food and forgiveness. Think about the day ahead and ask him to provide for you where necessary.

'And lead us not into temptation.' Pray for God's grace and strength in the various situations that you will find yourself in. Pray for wisdom and insight. Pray for guidance in knowing how to react in a particular situation. As you do so, you may find that you will have to revise your plans. Some you may have to drop because they are not right. Others you may have to phase in because God wants them done. When you act on God's guidance you will find that God honours you.

So spend some time each day praising God's glory, praying for God's goodness and asking for God's grace.

'Call to me and I will answer you and tell you great and unsearchable things you do not know' (*Jeremiah 33:3*).

'Seven days without prayer make one weak' (*Anonymous*).

> **If the thunder cloud passes rain, so let it rain, let it rain on me.**

Church

If you are a Christian you are part of the family of God. So don't go it alone, because you will lose your spirituality. St Augustine once said, 'We cannot have God as our father if we refuse to have the church for our mother.'

Belonging to a church (particularly a small group within the church), will bring you into touch with a variety of people who know the same Jesus. None of us Christians is perfect, but we are part of a family in which other believers can help us by their maturity and experience. You have a lot to learn and the church has a lot to learn from you.

In a church you will be able to worship – to give expression to the joy that is in your heart. And you will be able to receive teaching to stimulate your mind, to inspire you and to nourish you.

The church is not a cruise liner on which we glide into heaven. It is a battleship that requires all hands on deck as it fights its way through life to a tremendous destination. So get involved!

You may be experiencing a whole range of feelings. It is important that you reflect on the implications of the step you have taken, particularly in the area of sexual behaviour. You will have to explain to your friends what you have done. Don't worry, though, because if they are real friends they should accept you as you, Christian or not. You may sometimes feel disappointed as you see other Christians who don't live up to what you see as Christian standards (tell them off!), but don't give up on them.

. . . part of a family in which others can help us.

'Go for it!'

(Twentieth-century proverb)